The man
who shook
hands

By Diane Wakoski

The man
who shook
hands

DIANE WAKOSKI

Doubleday & Company, Inc.
Garden City, New York
1978

Looking for the bald eagles in Wisconsin was privately printed in *The Wandering Tatler*, copyright © 1975 by Diane Wakoski. Published by Perishable Press.

The last poem of the year . . . was privately published as a New Year's greeting by Black Sparrow Press, copyright © 1976 by Diane Wakoski.

The pumpkin pie was privately published as a Christmas greeting by Black Sparrow Press, copyright © 1972 by Diane Wakoski.

Peter Quince at the Clavier, copyright 1923 and renewed 1951, by Wallace Stevens. Reprinted from *The Collected Poems of Wallace Stevens*, by permission of Alfred A. Knopf, Inc.

The ring, Tearing up my mother's letters, and *The hitchhikers* were first published in *Poetry*, June 1977. Copyright © 1977 by The Modern Poetry Association.

Running men was published in *The Cornell Review*, copyright © 1977 by Cornell University.

The blue swan, an essay on music in poetry was first published in *A Shout in the Street*, Vol. I, No. 3, copyright © 1977 by Queens College Press.

ISBN: 0-385-13407—x Trade
ISBN: 0-385-13408—8 Paperbound
Library of Congress Catalog Card Number 77–80917

Contents

Introduction

To My Readers:

I begin this book of poems with an essay because it is a key to the book. However, not to the poems but only to where my philosophies and meditations are leading me. I wrote the essay, which is really about the use of digression as a structure, after about five months of listening to the recently released Folkways record of Charles Olson reading his work, and thinking, pondering, ruminating on the artist as a kind of archaeologist as well as the notion which I read in an essay by Robert Creeley about ten years ago proposing that, in twentieth-century literature, digression is often used as a structure and thus is not the traditional flaw in writing we often think it to be.

"The man who shook hands" has become a totemic figure, an obsession of mine, someone constantly present in my attempt to understand the world, and the essay is an attempt to show you the process of making an idea into music. The only apology I will offer for putting an essay at the beginning of a collection of poems is that you cannot hear me read it, for it was written to be read aloud, and it is definitely a theme and variations. I would like simply to say that some of the poets who have left their music in my head are, of course, Wallace Stevens and Charles Olson, but also Robert Duncan, Robert Kelly, Clayton Eshleman, Jerome Rothenberg, Frank O'Hara, and Galway Kinnell. It is with gratitude I acknowledge my musical debts. For everything else, I take full responsibility.

Sincerely,
DIANE WAKOSKI

I

The man who shook hands

Music is feeling, then, not sound;
And thus it is that what I feel,
Here in this room, desiring you,

Thinking of your blue-shadowed silk,
Is music.
. . . .

Beauty is momentary in the mind—
The fitful tracing of a portal;
But in the flesh it is immortal.

WALLACE STEVENS, from *Peter Quince at the Clavier*

The blue swan, an essay on music in poetry

Dear DAVID and ANNETTE,

Another remarkable weekend with you, embodying both our friendship over the years and the excitement, for me, of beginning to understand the nuances of aging. The perfection of both the momentary and the eternal. Do I sound sentimental and foolish? I don't mean to be. You are both such realists; as opposed to my pragmatism. Tom Thompson, my Boswell, said to me in amazement last winter—who knows after what incident or non-incident of my life he had witnessed—"You really do live in your imagination most of the time. I don't understand how you can do it." Yet, there is no great secret. When you are denied the life you want, you invent one for yourself. Unless you have no spirit. I am not a realist. For realistically what am I? Not a beautiful, slender, tan beachgirl Cinderella, but a short, stocky, usually pale, plain woman. I am not so much brilliant, as painfully acute and intelligent. I am not a performer, but a reactor. And yet I dream of being brilliant and amazing and powerful, aggressive, a center of attention. If I were a realist I would have to teach myself to abandon these foolish (and superficial) dreams. But I am not a realist. I am a pragmatist. I have learned to live with both my dreams and my reality. My dreams are the mythic me. Who is practically Mrs. America in the ordinariness of her dreams. The real me is a purveyor of dreams, a teacher of reality, a lover of music, knowing that "beauty is momentary in the mind—the fitful tracing of a portal; but in the flesh it *is* immortal." So, I dream of the flesh. Dream, the spirit, the poem. The flesh, its muse, its source, its proof, its "angle of repose." I could no more give up my idea of finding the perfect man than give up poetry. Are they not the same concept, the same spirit, the same holy quest, for beauty, embodied in the flesh, not denying, but attesting to the spiritual life?

And when I argued with you so passionately and loud, Annette, about your refusing to see me as aging, about your saying that it was my vision of myself which kept the perfect man from coming along or refusing to accept me if, in fact, he came along at all, and my shouting no, no, no, it is me, the aging body, the heavy face, which, in fact, makes serious men of all ages want to talk to me but *not* to make love to me/ digression/ a structure/ thank you Olson, thank you Creeley/ digression, a form of music, for music is that movement which we follow, that sound which we recognize not because it says anything but because it is motion which suspends motion, which does not ask for dialogue or response—digression which leads me to that serious proposition, that understanding of poetry, of talk, of the speech that comes from all of our lips, those words we call poetry, or dialogue, or digression, or discussion—can they pass into music?—and makes me ask if to speak seriously is not the most serious form of making love? Or does this question push me back into the centuries of American history where we understand thus from European history that "to make love" to a woman is to ask her to marry you, to speak beautiful forms of address/ digression, I plead with you; do you serve me well?

I want to address the body, which is the immortal. The idea, which is momentary in the mind. I want to discuss poetry, that body which will last so long as anyone wants it to. And the real body, which scarcely comes into existence with any awareness of itself and is lost before any serious use can be put to that awareness.

Let us start with the motif of "the man who shook hands." My year is so empty of music, I must start with primitive sounds. Everyone who knows me well—those few of you—know the story of the man who shook hands. Digression, stand aside. Now let me tell the story of the man who shook hands.

Once upon a time, there was an old witch whom everyone in town was afraid of. She was not a particularly powerful witch. Didn't know how to make unfaithful lovers fall in love with pigs. Didn't know how to make Cadillacs or loaves of bread stick to the fingers or feet of greedy people. Didn't know how to build a gingerbread house (it always crumbled before she got the roof glued on). Rather a failure, I'd say, as a witch. But she was the sort of person who knew a lot, lived alone and in an isolated manner, was neither beautiful nor fashionable and often scared people shitless with her expectations of them. Make her a witch in modern terms.

I hope you understand that all of this is digression and not very useful. Why don't I take it out and start over?

Okey. I'll start over. *The nature of music is that you must hear all the digressions.* For they are sometimes called variations, and they are sometimes called overtures, and in fact, I think you can probably think of some other names for them. Do you still think this is a radical theory? I think it is conventional. But like the witch, we have traditional predilections. But surely, by now, you are noticing the structures?

Second attempt at the story of the man who shook hands. Preliminary analysis. For more than two months I have lived with an explosive set of feelings which my rational mind cannot defend or even admire. I cannot let myself be outraged at something which most people (even I, when rational mind is applied) would think is silly. This is the same dilemma I had when I saw that clump of gigantic mushrooms on the lawn outside my office at the University of Virginia and was so overwhelmed with the beauty, the perfection, the sensuous, lustful feelings they aroused in me, that I spent a whole month keeping it a secret that I had seen them, and then wrote a poem about the process of knowing that no one would believe how beautiful they were, or conversely how it was important to me that I convey to someone how beautiful I *thot* they were.

Yet, our times encourage appreciation of the world of nature, and thus confession to my awe at the mushrooms (and adding other aesthetic experiences to the acknowledgment) is at least acceptable. What troubled me so much about the man who shook hands is culturally unacceptable, for *it blends the cool and the passionate in a way that everyone thinks trivial.* Even I think my reactions are foolish. Yet, it is on my mind:

Music is feeling, then, not sound;
And thus it is that what I feel,
Here in this room, desiring you,

Thinking of your blue-shadowed silk,
Is music.

The last stanza of that wonderful poem goes,

Susanna's music touched the bawdy strings
Of those white elders; but, escaping,
Left only Death's ironic scraping.
Now, in its immortality, it plays
On the clear viol of her memory,
And makes a constant sacrament of praise.

Third attempt at the story of the man who shook hands. Digression has led me to the bourgeois dilemma of art: how to speak of the deep things which concern, when you know, either, that they are not cosmic concerns or when you are not willing to attest to all the facts because they concern your feelings or responses to people who do not feel or respond the same way you do. People who may be sitting in front of you listening to you speak. People who may read the books you print. Who may take your words and turn them into taunts, explosions, arguments, symbols of your foolishness or meanness.

Once upon a time, there was a princess from another fable who'd been through a lot of trouble. She was that princess who spoke poetry and who was kidnaped. Lost her diamond pencil, etc. All that stuff about people who didn't like poetry but liked the princess who spoke poetry and gradually found that they rather liked a world in which someone spoke poetry. Evil astronomers. Usual rotten politics. All that fairy-tale crap.

Anyway, this princess who spoke poetry discovered that,
after a while, a lot of people spoke poetry. And she herself
fell in love with

Wait a minute, Wakoski. This is Digression taking over. I don't
know what you think you're doing with these boring serial fairy
tales. A serial detective, maybe. But surely not a serial princess.
You are not chic enough to be the Mary Hartman of the poetry
world. What about this character: the man who shook hands. Who
ever heard of anybody shaking hands with a princess? Don't they
kneel and kiss her hand or put glass slippers on her foot or
something? And what's this blue swan in your title? And where's
all this music you said you'd be talking about. This is page 6. I
want some action.
    Fourth attempt at the story of the man who shook hands.
(Wakoski, listen to me, you are getting to the point of diminishing
returns. By now, everybody is expecting a pretty good story and, so
far as I can see, the only reason why you haven't told us the whole
story up front is that you think it's not such a hot story.
    Sir, the reason I have not told this story to any but my closest
friends is that it is a trivial story which makes me seem like a
foolish person for even seeing the incident as a story. If the anecdote
(as opposed to story) could be casually mentioned and then
brushed off as an allusion to the ironic fate of foolish lovers, then
it might be rather a lily trailing around a big old volume of
interesting stories. A little echo of deceit and foolishness. A slight
sound of trumpet in the background to reinforce the theme with
some augmenting sadness about the world. But, as a story, it's
strictly second rate. And the fact that my life is such that I could
make it a story testifies not that I live in my imagination but that
I am scarcely alive.
    All right, Wakoski, you get one more chance at the story,
without digressions, at which point you'd better do something with

it. Remember those beautiful words, "music, is feeling, then, not sound. . . ."

Fifth attempt at the story of the man who shook hands. Oh, my god, I guess I'd better tell you directly and get it over with. How, how can I convince you that it will mean anything? Context? Setting? Period? Oh, my god, I'm not even a storyteller. I've already told you what has run away with my imagination, like the dish with the spoon—that this man shook hands with me.

Wakoski,

Okey. Okey. First you have to read my curriculum vitae.

Wakoski, is this a story or a testimony? What happened? Did you get religion? Shake hands with God?

No, no, forgive me. All right. This is difficult for me because it is autobiographical. And my response is both a horrified realization of self I did not suspect and an anger at the world for seeing the physical me, not the poetic or metaphysical me. Please let me have a little dignity in this story. Dignity lies in the spirit. The body can seldom provide a paradigm for it. But if "Beauty is momentary in the mind," what gives the mind beauty's clue?

May I be permitted a digression about the body? About sex? About its vexing lack of harmony with love, the sense of romance, and the spirit?

No; you're supposed to be writing about that in *Greed: Part 10*. Get on with the story.

Okey, may I preface my remarks with the traditional "All characters and events in this story are purely fictional and any relation to real events or people is purely coincidental"?

No.

Wakoski, I thot you just wrote an essay on revision. Why are you fucking around like this? Are you waiting for some other writer's muse?

Sixth attempt at the story of the man who shook hands:
While waiting for the King of Spain, many things may happen to a poet. She might, in fact, meet an economist, a chemist, or even a specialist in soybeans. She might meet one of the few people who had a piece of George Ohr pottery, one of his puzzle mugs or an inkwell in the shape of a log cabin. Henry James himself might have left a great-great-grandnephew who sails and tucks her into the cabin with the jib for a windy day. She might take up tennis or be involved in espionage with a graduate of a fine liberal arts college like Whitman. But whatever happens, you cannot take it too seriously, for you must know that she is simply whiling away her time, as well as possible, waiting, yes waiting, for the King of Spain.

Seventh attempt at the story of the man who shook hands.

The acts are simple. The narrative is complicated, for it is the story of someone who has loved and loved and loved, but unsuccessfully. Someone who does not want you to sympathize with foolish love. Someone who regards the act as inevitable, yet wishes to make it thoughtful and exceptional. As art. As poetry. As music. There is only one reason why you could sympathize with this story, and it is that you must care for the terrible lack of reciprocity we all must learn to live with. If you have not yet felt it, let me only say I love and envy you for your incompleteness. And of course, that inevitably you will feel it, as we all feel death, not as punishment, but simply the inevitable.

Lack of reciprocity. Is it a history? Is it experienced by those who are insensitive or unresponding to others? I don't know any answers. But would only say that if you are tempted to easy ones,

I hope you will understand that that ease will itself someday betray you. I want you to love and feel your love reciprocated. I only preface this story to say that reciprocity is the exception. Not the rule.

And, of course, this story is not even about love. It is not even about the mistakes of love. It is about lust. Need. Pleasure. Its accompaniment: pain.

We will start with a woman. One approaching middle age. One who loves beauty. One who is silent often. One who speaks as an act of beauty. One who believes that "beauty is momentary in the mind—the fitful tracing of a portal; but in the flesh it is immortal."

We will start with not me but my vision of me. We will start with a woman who regards herself as desirable. Who is in love and looking for the perfect exponent of it. We are looking at a woman who trusts all the natural processes and believes that love naturally transforms everything alive. We are looking at a woman who found the right man and lost him. Who does not know why this happened, for all the while she was happy he was unhappy. So we are looking at an ordinary woman. One living in the natural non-reciprocal world, trying hard to believe in reciprocity, trying to shoulder the burden for lack of correspondence, trying still to find not love nearly so much as reciprocity.

> *Music is feeling, then, not sound;*
> *And thus it is that what I feel,*
> *Here in this room, desiring you,*
>
> *Thinking of your blue-shadowed silk,*
> *Is music.*

I met a man. I could have been at the ends-of-the-earth. We both had empty, isolated lives. I disliked him the first time I met him. I thought he was rather stupid. I thought he was a phony. And I knew that people, at that terrible ends-of-the-earth, would try to pair us up because we were both longhairs and we were both single.

I managed to avoid him. But I also began to realize that I was at the ends-of-the-earth and that maybe no one else was there. An occasion arose when we two got together. He still seemed not so much stupid as silly to me. Perhaps because I was older. But since I have been married to several men ten years younger than I (and whatever failed in our relationships, age was not the villain), age did not seem a problem. And one of the propositions which become more and more important to me is the value of a complex nature. I cannot bear superficiality, simple-mindedness, or people who refuse to yield to their deeper natures. This man seemed determined to pursue fashion and not at all concerned with the ideas underneath it. He thot he was brilliant, radical, unusual, and unique. I thot he was ordinary, foolish, doctrinaire, and just another young man of fashion. However, remembering that "beauty is momentary in the mind"—and the man I loved was far away and determined never to see me again—"the fitful tracing of a portal; but in the flesh it is immortal," I went the way of all flesh. Found that he might be an ordinary and foolish man but he was a good lover.

And yes, I am a pragmatist. I found myself excited by the idea that this man and I, both stuck at the ends-of-the-world for a few months, would relieve each other's physical discomfort. I felt old and wise enough to carry on a relationship without burdening it with a future or with fairy-tale endings. I felt, also, that maybe this impossible man would become the perfect man. I felt excited by many impossibilities.

Well, by now you must know the ending. Foreshadowing. . . . God, I've hit you over the head with the inevitable. The next day, when he left, he did not do anything I expected. After a comfortable morning together, he announced he had to go home and work. That seemed reasonable to me. But as he left, he did not embrace me, as lovers embrace, just out of physical excitement or satisfaction. He, yes, you know it all by now. *He shook my hand.* I cannot tell you how that physically shocked me. I cannot tell you what that did to my image of love, sex, reality, or myself. I believe for an instant he saw my startled (terrified?) reaction, and I, because I am small and a woman and used to embracing those I care for, moved toward him and embraced him. Not he me. He left, and I have never seen him since. So there it is: the sad, silly, not very important, yet overwhelmingly terrifying story of the man who shook hands. A silly story, because those who like me say, "Diane, you know that story is simply a commentary on how shallow and superficial he was" and those who do not like me say that it is proof that we all get what we deserve, and to me it is an endless terrified question, continuing from a long terrible story of the question: how can I love, enjoy, or care about someone and find that he either does not love, enjoy, or care about me? Is is possible that I can find someone very attractive and he find me repulsive? Annette, you argued that whatever the man who shook hands felt, it was not repulsion. Perhaps it was realization of a discrepancy in our lives or simply a formal feeling that if I wanted the situation renewed, I should initiate it. Yet, as a traditional woman (substitute *poet*), I felt that I had offered myself and been formally rejected. "Although your material has much to recommend it, we find it unsuitable for our publication." "Your poems have many attractive qualities but the editors are not finally persuaded." "You have not read our magazine or you would not have sent us these poems." "This material is not for us." "Would you be interested in subscribing to our magazine, which publishes America's finest authors? Perhaps reading it would give you some hints for self-development and growth."

Now that I have told you this story and revealed the vanity of my obsessions, I want to try to address myself to the final question of music, and why "in the flesh" it *is* "immortal"? Why, if such silly stories can show us the basic silliness of the act we all regard as sacred, why should I, who have devoted my life to intelligent action, the beautiful use of language, the truly radical as opposed to the silly or easy fashion, why should I care about a man whom from the beginning I not only did not notice as having any spiritual values but whom I also did not have one of those physical cravings for. Your son, David Jr., the delightful surfer, hero of his high school shop classes, fabled lover of teen-age girls—he has always physically fascinated and attracted me, and thank god for my elderly age difference, for out of dignity, no matter how sexy or beautiful, I would not chase your son. He is, after all, almost the age of my own son. But here I am, stewing, not only physically but metaphysically, about a man who in no way is my vision of the perfect man. Doing this after years of *not* fretting about why men I actually loved or was fascinated by did not love me. Am I stewing because he presents a powerful case to refute my interest in the perfect man? Does he prove that all of my life is not myth or allegory or even poetry, but some very long and complicated soap opera of pragmatism.

I would not be honest if I did not face that possibility. And it has obsessed me for months now. Yet, I will not give in so easily to critics who wish to reduce my poetry (read "life") to foolish soap opera. *I think I am obsessed with the man who shook hands because I did, for the first time, encounter someone who wished to try formally to explain that terrible subject—lack of reciprocity —to me.* And I hang on to my image of pale face in yellow kimono being asked to shake hands with a man, an act that suddenly changes the meaning of my thoughts for the preceding twelve hours. One act to change hours of observation and seemingly perception. And, Annette, I will not accept your absolution of my painful thoughts, for while you are right that he probably was not

thinking, "What a repulsive woman! How could I have spent the
night with her?" he was probably thinking, "How different from
me she is. How could I have spent the night (substitute two years,
ten months, or two weeks) with her?" And does it make any
difference ultimately when such a thing is said? For the act of
saying it cancels out whatever period of time went before it. And
it means that one side of perception is invalidated, while another
side of it is invested with history. And I, the perceiver, the poet,
I am the one who is invalidated. So now we do not have a man
rejecting a woman. You are all right. How common. But we have a
poet perceiving reality and within twelve hours being told her
perceptions are completely wrong.

Well, I did not write this essay to appease Marjorie Perloff
and other critics who are looking for cases to add validity to their
already final condemnation of my poetry. And since this is not a
poem, I feel that any fuel they add to their fires from this essay
ought to burn greasy and polluting. But this is an essay for those
of you—David and Annette—who love me, and for those of you
whom, reciprocally, I do love (and there can be no doubt of that).
And it is an essay into origins, modes, and then styles. For first
comes the story. Then comes the reaction to the story. Then
come the telling and retelling of the story. And finally, David, as
you have pointed out to me, comes boredom with the story, so that
finally we invent music, and the nature of music is that you must
hear all the digressions. And while I do not claim to have done that
in this essay, I claim to have given you the process for reaching
that music. If a stranger is reading this piece and wishes to end
with my own music, I invoke him to recite *Blue Monday* or *The
Pink Dress* or a poem such as *The Magellanic Clouds* in my voice
or his own. But since I am speaking this piece today for those
whom I care about, I will render the whole of Wallace Stevens'
wonderful *Peter Quince at the Clavier*.

Just as my fingers on these keys
Make music, so the selfsame sounds
On my spirit make a music, too.

Music is feeling, then, not sound;
And thus it is that what I feel,
Here in this room, desiring you,

Thinking of your blue-shadowed silk,
Is music. It is like the strain
Waked in the elders by Susanna.

Of a green evening, clear and warm,
She bathed in her still garden, while
The red-eyed elders watching, felt

The basses of their beings throb
In witching chords, and their thin blood
Pulse pizzicati of Hosanna.

In the green water, clear and warm,
Susanna lay.
She searched
The touch of springs,
And found
Concealed imaginings.
She sighed,
For so much melody.

Upon the bank, she stood
In the cool
Of spent emotions,
She felt, among the leaves,
The dew
Of old devotions.

She walked upon the grass,
Still quavering.
The winds were like her maids,
On timid feet,
Fetching her woven scarves,
Yet wavering.

A breath upon her hand
Muted the night.
She turned—
A cymbal crashed,
And roaring horns.

III

Soon, with a noise like tambourines,
Came her attendant Byzantines.

They wondered why Susanna cried
Against the elders by her side;

And as they whispered, the refrain
Was like a willow swept by rain.

Anon, their lamps' uplifted flame
Revealed Susanna and her shame.

And then, the simpering Byzantines
Fled, with a noise like tambourines.

IV

Beauty is momentary in the mind—
The fitful tracing of a portal;
But in the flesh it is immortal.

The body dies; the body's beauty lives.
So evenings die, in their green going,
A wave, interminably flowing.
So gardens die, their meek breath scenting
The cowl of winter, done repenting.
So maidens die, to the auroral
Celebration of a maiden's choral.

Susanna's music touched the bawdy strings
Of those white elders; but, escaping,
Left only Death's ironic scraping.
Now, in its immortality, it plays
On the clear viol of her memory,
And makes a constant sacrament of praise.

No, I cannot end this essay with Stevens, for the nature of music,
as I have said, is that you must hear all the digressions. And my
theme, the man who shook hands, has not quite been revealed yet.
So, risking banishment from Arthur's court, where all knights
questing for the Sangreal return to tell their tales of adventure,
and risking the sneers of Madame Perloff or Monseiur Bloom, I
am going to end with a poem of my own. It is called

The blue swan, an essay on music
in poetry

Olson, the poet as archaeologist,
sifting the dirt for pieces of pottery which might reveal
the conventions
between men and women.
He found a large piece of shaped clay
with what appeared
to be a blue swan
painted on it. And knowing
that there were no lakes or bodies of water
nearby, that waterfowl had not lived in that place in the memory of
    man,
he concluded that he had found something
coming from outside that culture, foreign, alien, yet beautiful
    enough
to be carried around, or perhaps something beautiful attached
to something useful,
the beauty not being noticed. The pot being used for daily rations
of water, its blue swan floating
on terra cotta, a lake of singular density and
not real.

Floating on terra cotta, a lake
of singular density and not real.
The blue swan floating
on terra cotta, a lake of singular density and not real.
The moon has no telephone number
to be called in the radical night.
But poetry, music,
they come out of the body, the lips, like terra cotta, showing the

painted blue swan,
an emblem of something coming from outside
the world where such waterfowl float in relative cool,
or perhaps reminding that a desert was once an ocean,
the shock of knowing something different,
this history of discrepancies,
including that greatest one—why a man and woman do not
    simultaneously love and enjoy each other.

I wonder if he looked at me
and, instead of a body, saw all of civilization,
instead of hands and lips, a tall, smooth water vase painted with
    water lilies
and all the wild swans of Coole,
broken into shards;
if he saw the archaeologists digging,
sifting through history for an understanding of daily life,
and in Olson's hand,
a piece of shaped clay, with what appeared to be a blue swan
    painted
on it, and that hand
was my hand,
my lips were sealed against time.
He took the hand and shook it.
Why should I cry or feel hurt? Why should this terrify me
or break my heart?
Because I am not history, only one of its digressions?
In history,
women and men do not shake hands.

                                                yrs,
                                          DIANE

Running men

How touching: the image of Hemingway guiding Fitzgerald
through the Louvre
to show him how small the genitals of all men
are,
    that he wasn't a freak, or even inadequate,
as his wife had made him think.

And I, wandering through the Met to convince myself
my own figure is not a total failure,
only to find
that my legs are
too short for the rest of me,
as I've always known;
that,
being reinforced by a sculptor who, in making my body, gave me
    height,
and of course,
lengthened my legs.

But here I am,
with no kind old man to reassure me,
thinking of my short, stubby legs, no longer an item of trivia
but a measure of falling short of classical standards.

Facing failure,
while the bloom of a phalaenopsis shadows my hand,
and winter sunlight floods in over the keyboard,
and I continue to admit
how much I must live in my imagination.

The man who shook hands with me, after making love,
the last rung in some ladder to failure
I've been descending.
                    (Where was Orpheus really going
                        when he searched for Eurydice?)
Winter thoughts. Accompanied by Schumann and a pot of
    Darjeeling.
I sit and think of how others use their legs.
The men running.
The women dancing.
And I, simply sitting here, on my short legs, their only advantage
    that they permit me
to travel in relative comfort.

The image of you, standing at my front door, in grey track suit,
tall,
with long legs,
and I holding myself back for fear of betraying my feelings,
my sad silly short-legged honest body, which, like its father,
can tell no lies.
How it would betray what I feel. So, I stand,
stiff, and pull my head back as we embrace. Parting,
Only because of myth do you not, also, offer to shake my hand.

And the image of a friend, a poet, showing up sweaty one evening
when I was visiting a friend in New York,
and I smiling at the contrast between him and you. He, so wispy
    and small,
with a pinched starving face, perhaps a short-order man in a diner,
while you, tall, young, robust, I imagine you running as a
    Schumann composition pulls
the fingers of Arturo Benedetti Michelangeli along the keyboard,
    tripling and
flexing each arc and bend of the various body.
Contrasts.

And another runner, blind and supple from winter skiing,
who jogs through Texas, the land of Beaujolais clouds
and domestic jaguars,
until he runs into the arteries which lead away from my heart,
away, running farther and farther until, in vain,
I think of running too.

A parody, these running men,
none of whom I really understand, perhaps because
most girls can't run.

The kindness of old man Hemingway, the care he felt for poor
    tormented Fitzgerald,
like the kindness of my own friends who insist that there is
    nothing wrong with me,
when I plainly see how much longer my legs (sic)
should be,
looking at any portrait or statue
in history; such pathetic realities. For, what good to his marriage
    did

the view in the Louvre do to Fitzgerald? Measures are imposed
    before we even know them
I think of you, standing at my door in the West,
your grey track suit like a uniform,
leaving me,
saying good-by,
New friends. Not ever to be lovers.
I, trying to guide myself through the museums of the world, teach
    myself
all the lessons life has pressed into my texts and never explained.
I, always wanting to touch,
but finally,
not being able to.
My body stiff and frightened,
turned into mineral, reflecting the grey cotton of your soft
track suit.

So many lessons.
First, that you must love in order to learn.
But no, the lessons we learn, we cannot,
we should not
tell.

I live with this image,
which sparks, and sends me running on:
you, at my door, in the West, wearing your grey track suit,
and I stiff, afraid of myself, leaning away
from what I want most.
Sensibly.
Wisely.
Taking with me the lesson you so gently taught in your kind
    final gesture,
that stiff embrace.

I live in my head.

The bodies in my life are the perfect ones of museums and art.

Let me touch you with poetry, for that is the only keyboard my
fingers really know.

Standing at the door

At the door,
we are saying good-by.
To the old, the young look very soft.
Like rabbits,
or deer,
the soft pets of children.
Thus, in your grey track suit,
though you are as tall as an oversized refrigerator, I see you
in the way we view
small, soft things.
Yet, we embrace a little like a small woman and a refrigerator,
two bodies made of such different materials,
each equally unyielding. Inappropriate.
Not matched.

An incredible silence in my life
has left me with this image.
One I keep turning over and over in my head.
Of the embrace which means nothing to you and which, to me,
is another sign of failure.
You have not shaken my hand, at least.
A gesture I have been horrified by
since a lover departed, shaking my hand, not saying
another word.
Yet, we are not lovers.
And should not be. Why do I think of you,
my student,

in your grey track suit,
tall, blond, from the same little town in Southern California where
    I grew up,
a young and very nice man,
who understands kindness perhaps better than any man I've ever
    known,
or at least is willing to show it truly,
as few men are?
And I, perhaps as shocked by kindness as by a lover
shaking my hand,
freeze
that moment in which I wanted you as a lover more than anything
    in the world.
Freeze it,
with my stiff body,
like one of the bodies in all of those murder mysteries I read,
leaning away from you,
afraid to touch your kindness.

In retrospect, I have to realize
how false the linking of sex with violence is
for most women.
For my body was alive with sexual feelings,
feelings that if I touched you,
I would melt into you,
like some foolish description out of *True Romance,*
and so I held back.
That moment frozen. Me, holding back,
stiff,
rigid,
a small person,
from your tall body in its grey track suit, and I know now
what I felt was love

for your kindness,
for that gentle concern you had really shown,
even the kindness
of being curious about the identity of the man who shook hands.

We did share a sexual drama.
And I was not the teacher then,
or you my student.
You taught me that men can be kind,
loving,
and gentle. And you did not desert me
when you left me,
though I have not seen you since.
Your gesture was one of loving, not leaving.
Making up, finally, for
the man who shook hands.
Teaching me my own responses are true.
Reciprocity a puzzle for us all.

I think of you,
tall as a refrigerator,
and wonder if I unconsciously think of you as cold;
know that my interpretation is wrong.
You, a preserver, like the best Frigidaire,
and I,
you allow me to continue with faith in this world where chilling
    preserves,
prevents spoilage and waste,
where it gives continuity,
my favorite Meursault chilled for its best fragrance,
and the low temperatures my most beautiful plants
thrive in.

Love poem to Leon Edel &
Ross MacDonald

The terrible truth
is that we write our own histories.
Poets die young.
Novelists, like Henry James, attend 107 dinner parties in one
  season.
Detectives rescue our daydreams.
Universities pay our salaries.
A bottle of good red bordeaux and an orchid.
That's all I require for nirvana.

Gentlemen:
the act of love ought to be a private one.
Yet, I have had nothing but trouble out of my private acts.
Surely, if history were accurate
I should be in love with both of you,
since George Washington hovers over my shoulder while I type,
Freud reads my letters,
and recently Jung has been making phone calls.
Along with all this,
I grow healthy begonias, dedicate them to Stevens,
and when drinking, always pour an extra glass for my own
  particular Elijah, Mr. Yeats.

Homage, then, I must be talking about.
For love has always been the process of sacrificing something
for a good fuck. In my life, at least. And I have always sanctioned
  marriage

39

(still do) because it's the only way a woman can have a dignified
     sex life.
Yet, here I am, unmarried.
With, of course, no sex life.
And wondering what love is all about.
Thus, I write a love letter, to two men,
both of whom are happily married and not interested in a woman
     who steps on the moon's
sliver
to take the broken step
in life's perfect dance.
But, surely, poetry opens some doors?
How various, the acts of the imagination.

> I have a fiction-writing student who has no imagination; yet,
> she insists on her heroine's having an imaginary dog.
> Whatever virtues her writing has, one of them is not the
> ability to make any reader believe in an imaginary dog.
> Yet, like a real dog with a bone, she will not give up her
> imaginary dog. It proves she has imagination.

> I spent a night with a man who, upon leaving, shook hands
> with me. I have not recovered from the shock yet.

> I met a student who was so beautiful I felt lust. He wanted
> to shake my hand when he left me, but knowing of my
> shock, he tried to embrace me. I was frightened, and for
> the first time realized that I was afraid of my own feelings.
> Writing about reality had put me out of touch with them.
> Feelings are not part of reality.

I can make anything grow, but when I go away everything
dies.

I married a man who confused me.

I married a second man who confused me. Even after I had
discovered what confused me about the first one. The second
confusion concerned fiction, an act of the imagination.
I know a number of men who interest me, but they are more
interested in slim hips than in reality. Why have we all paid
so much attention to the physical? It has done nothing to help
the cause of the living.

Thus, the sun goddess tried to contain her fire:

I spent the weekend with Rilke.
Only set one thing on fire.

Once, he said to me, "This is not the customary cigarette,"
his black mustache curling through the smoke,
my white body characeous,
a water lily in his grandmother's Old World garden.

No more so this,
the customary love letter.
I wish you alone
to be
one of many.

When you have time,
meet me at the Coral Casino,

past the sea anemones, triggers, clowns and angels.
In the presence of both your devils and the beautiful women you
  must leave behind
when you come to talk
to me.

The King of Spain discovered as a Mexican bandit

Standing
next to me
you
first become lilting Rilke. But then your mustache
grows,
and poetry turns into pistols
the bandits come out of the hills,
my shoulders so white they could be the lilies of easter,
risen,
"Buenos dias, Señor,"

Seeing that you speak in a foreign language,
and counting the crows in the sky,
I think,
think,
"surely someday the mustache will be white,"
and then then
words will be stronger
more vivid
than the images of convented girls
like little white breviaries.

Don't pluck that one white hair in your sooty mustache, *Señor*.
It is the beginning of your age,
where words come first,
the body lamely trailing.
That age belongs to me.

Thinking of Rilke's mustache while writing to the man in Receiving at Sears

The locust tree is feathering itself into spring outside this window.
Somewhere in the past, buried like a root,
the mustache of Pancho Villa turns lustrous and thick,
as if it too were expanding with luscious spring. I remember his
    hands,
Rilke's, that is,
and of course the jet black scythes of his mustache
I cling to them,
strong, tough, like alpine growth jutting out of the crags
of this rocky place,
keeping my balance, holding on for dear
life,
looking down over the green world.

It is more blessed to give
than to receive
in certain dogmas. Yet, I bless you
for waiting to receive me,
hanging perilously from the rocks I have chosen to climb.
No pitons. Only
Rilke's mustache
tenuously holding me there, still balanced, wondering,
wondering,
about the lights of the cities spread out under me,
a million porch lights
left on,
for late husbands, wives,
returning travelers.
Or travelers who might never return.

A warning to the man in Receiving at Sears

Be suspicious,
I say,
of this woman who singles you out as her favorite correspondent.
Blithely,
you load up the mails with packages,
stack boxes on your trolley at Sears,
stand at your break thinking of ice cream sundaes,
and stop off after work to visit the local framer. What, I wonder, do
you make of my preference for you
while reminiscing over Mr. Minimal or Rilke whose black mustache
   still
makes me faint with desire,
just to see one of my own amateurish photos.

And why do you think
just because you've stopped asking *yourself* why,
that there might not be any reason
for things you find hard to explain?

What makes you think
life is as simple as a frame house in Trenton, New Jersey,
a job in Receiving at Sears,
Saturday photographs, and fishing,
the long nights of poetry and letters?

You must think, like reflects like. Or things breed themselves.
Or even, that there is no alchemy beyond, perhaps,
baseball games and big fishing trips.

Let me tell you,
that some fish spawn up crazy streams and turn into fantastic
    things.
We have salmon and trout because they were seeded by the
    government.
In real life, things come together and create fearful combinations.
Letters do not breed letters.
Poems, poems.
Even television sets do not spawn little RCA colour sets.
No,
poets
did not make up griffons,
or hippogriffs.
Nor did we make up love, the crazy combinations
of woodworker and poet.

YES, be a
little suspicious,
I say,
not really of me. Old toothless lion.
But,
I laughed when a girl told me I was talking dangerously,
speaking of "The Special View of History," but
I know that there is danger when there is something you are not
    prepared for.
And so I say,
simply remember, like does not breed like.
You think you have a simple life.
Is it as simple as you want it?

Yes, be suspicious,
for it will be you who suddenly finds himself appalled
at how large the multiples become

even,
with one and one.

The photograph in the letter

Sometimes I remember putting my fingers on the keyboard
in the chord formation of G major or D.
One by one, each finger
like the finches who land on the feeder,
one by one, until there is a chord of them, G major, D,
C, sometimes, then, a cluster of them,
with variously stained, juicy coloured heads.
A chipping sparrow might be near by,
or a fox, their rusty colours
in the grey morning starting to move towards the purple
and red of the other little birds' heads.

Your letter comes
this time on long paper,
perhaps an indication of how much you want to say,
perhaps an indication of how much space there always is
around the few words we do find for each other.

In my memory,
it is always chords,
and often the finding of them,
the notes discovered one by one. Sometimes I wish
I were Cecil Taylor,
could, at least in memory, lay my arms across the keyboard
definitively,
powerfully,

taking whole rows of tones in my arms,
splashing them out into the air,
making the whole keyboard mine.

And if memory can be an act of invention,
why, then, can't I take my small hands with their imprint of
    chords
singly formed, lift them up, attach them to my sturdy arms which,
    like Wanda Landowska's,

once were very beautiful, and in memory, or invention of memory,
move those arms in bold patterns of noise,
proclamation,
joy?

Only, I suppose, because I am not Beethoven,
or any of those great performers.
A passionate reader of letters,
sitting each morning at my desk,
watching the finches,
this morning a Steller Jay, and on the roof next door, a common
    robin.
Loving the long paper on which you sent your letter,
looking at the photos which come in letters,
of Rilke,
the man in Receiving at Sears,
and now, The Skier,
tempted to think,
something is real
only if it is
on paper.

Overnight projects with wood

for all the plumbers, carpenters, & mechanics

Lined up
like chocolates in their perfect paper jackets,
the boys on one side of the room.
The girls,
little shelled filberts,
on the other;
The girls are going
to home economics for the first time.
And the boys,
to shop. To manual training.

But you thot "manual training" meant learning
to be a man.
And thus today you are a carpenter,
plumber,
mechanic,
woodsman.

I,
I knew that home economics
had nothing to do with being
a woman.

Now two friends speak to me.
Rilke, with his jet-black mustache curling like a scythe,
smiled this week as he told me he won a silver dollar in sixth
    grade
for building the best birdhouse.
His father, the tailor, had just built a house in Ohio,
and the wood, like scraps from a new suit,
fresh and unscarred, made a house
snug beyond the dreams of a poet.
When I see him,
he jingles the lonely silver dollar in his pocket,
a medal for his beautiful hands.
And he feels no need to build a house of his own.

The man from Receiving, at Sears,
did not begin his birdhouse until seventh grade.
And though his book promised this as an overnight project
this birdhouse required two years to become a
chaotic tower of babel.
Or, so he says.

I have all these stories from men,
while I remember my own perfect blanket stitch, and neat
    patching.
A good batch of biscuits.
Tho I rebelled against making a nice apron, cut a hole in the
    middle of it,
and mine was, thus, too disgraceful to be shown on parents' night.

Oh, we were all little ice-cream sundaes then;
butterfingers,
or creamy fudge.
Such babies,
such children,
thinking, dreaming,
You, of manhood,
Rilke and his brother, the man in Receiving at Sears,
training for wisdom.
I,
what was I doing?
Making my own perfect blanket stitch,
patching neatly,
making good biscuits,
And rebelling, rebelling, against a plain apron.

For the running man

You know the story,
the woman,
            as if frozen in stone, stiff in her chair,
and lifted to the sky, Cassiopeia,
sitting there with stars for each foot,
a straight-backed, glittering chair in the sky,

I can only look at you
from such a distance that if I could move,
(but I cannot move),
I could not touch you.

Longing.
Is it the most innocent form of love?
And the word,
the most complete
form
      of love?

I speak,
Or do I speak?
I withhold
some words. More perfect,
truer
for living
only in the mind. Human love:
that is imperfect.

The word,
sister,
sitting as our two-children portrait,
with you in red velvet and I in blue,
in starry chairs,
next to each other,
word and deed:
such disparate entities.

II

Life is like
a game of cards

Life is like a game of cards, or another one of those metaphysical statements from a distant reader

for Al Greenberg & Wendy Parish

I said to Alvin,
"I like to play games, even tho I never win.
I somehow feel that they reflect life,
and one thing poetry has taught me
how to do is embrace success when it comes,
while not getting too upset about failure."

He agreed with me.
Of course, secretly, he thought I would be
one of those people who won a lot but just
downplayed it.
Was he ever surprised when we played
three games of Oh Hell or Oh Pshaw, as it is sometimes called,
and he won all three. And, in fact,
I not only lost but came
nowhere near to winning.
But I enjoyed the games.
Drank a lot of cognac.
Ate popcorn.
Thought about how many things I was a failure at,
including love and marriage,
maybe even life.

How everyone is disappointed when they meet me,
because I really am ugly,
and I really am plain,
and I really am
fairly dull,
just as I've said
(to great rhetorical effect).
And every day I live with the knowledge
I've disappointed someone
who expected something better from me.
It's not true that people don't want to play cards with **you**
if you always win.
That actually challenges them.
What embarrasses them,
what they dread,
is to play with someone, like me,
who always loses,
usually good-naturedly,
hiding whatever chagrin I feel
somewhat successfully.

I call up Alvin and ask if he and Wendy
want to play cards again this Saturday.
"No," they say,
they have lots of work to do.
I sit at home and read.
I've always known the truth
about everything.
But I carry on.

Pain. Yes, isn't it a burden to get
from day to day?

But how to respect anyone
who willingly gives up that struggle?
Anne, Sylvia, John, Virginia,
you were cowards. I'll say it now,
and get it over with.
We all suffer.
It angers me to hear only those cowards who give up
spoken of as "sensitive."
How much more dignity, power,
we must have to carry on, precisely when it is
too painful.

When I was young, I also used to like to play games.
But my little sister, who was younger and perhaps not as smart,
always ruined the game by quitting
when she was losing.
It angered me so much once I tried to beat her to death.
Now I never see my sister. I still try to find people to play games
    with,
and I never quit when I am losing.
Tho, others so often seem to refuse to play,
as if they fear I will always win.
Alvin,
I don't understand the world.

I sit alone
in a garden of wild California poppies,
their simple silk leaves against a brown hillside,
waiting, waiting,
for the King of Spain,
knowing that fantasy lifts us all
beyond pain.

How do you tell a story?

The mask stares down at me,
round, open, frightened mouth, holding only three teeth,
an old grapefruit,
an old woman.
Myself,
seeing life,
as life sees me.

> When troubled with how to tell a
>   story,
> I remind myself of Aristotle's
>   procedure,
> Start at the beginning, my dear,
> and proceed to the middle. Conclude
> at the end, my dear. (You will
>   never be
> the emperor of ice-cream.)

But where is the beginning?
My anger with the ironies and pain of life?
Surely, an abstraction is not a beginning?
But if the beginning begins before the story began? What then?
Well, surely, Diane, Olson was there to pave the way?

> He was brave,
> but not the emperor of ice-cream.

I will be brave, then, too.
and tell you that I am moved by two things: beauty,
and injustice.

How *do* you tell the story of the man
who shook
hands?

The mask
is where I am sitting.
The story is what my mind is trying to construct.
The dialogue is what is interfering with the poem.
The poem
has not yet begun,
for a story must come first,
or there can be no poem.

The round, empty eyeholes,
the open mouth, as if to scream,
Where can I start,
that you will understand me? We only listen to
the very beautiful,
though sometimes the ugly man is allowed to scream at the door.

Yesterday,
sitting in a comfortable room,
a beautiful girl, with silver-blond hair to her waist,
tall, with a long oval face, her skin like expensive opals,
her lips perfect, neatly set, quietly closed,
her voice soft, her rhythms so slow
you could imagine she had been born playing the harpsichord,
she sat and told us that she was different from everyone
because she wrote poems.

Yet, every one of us in that room was a poet.
She was different only
because her body was so beautiful,
her face so serene,
her composure, so exceptional.

This beautiful moonstone of a girl
read a beautiful moonstone of a poem
in which she identified with a famous woman poet who was famous
    for being
hypersensitive and who suffered from giving poetry readings
and who, in fact, had recently died by her own automobile exhaust.
This pearly girl, a drink of Pernod,
accused her sensible mother of insensitivity
for, when told the story of the hypersensitive poet,
her mother replied, "Perhaps she should have had some other line
    of work
if giving readings troubled her so much."

This was considered an insensitive, even devastating thing
to have said.

                              Why do we consider "sensitivity"
                              a virtue in humans,
                              when it is the hardest stone
                              which is considered the most
                                  valuable?
                              Surely, it is the intelligence to
                                  survive,
                              not the outwitting softness
                              we should honor?

You see, I get bogged down in both narrative and comment.
For the real story is of my own horror
at life,
every moment of which is almost too painful to live,
and my anger at this softness;
the truth I see,
which only allows human dignity
if you *do* carry on, if you do teach yourself to be somewhat gracious
under your burdens. And I think of the lady in question,
who did not, in fact, have to give poetry readings,
who was, in fact, moderately wealthy, who had,
in fact, already won many honors in that stingy world of poetry
and who could only have had one reason for doing something so
    painful to her
that it made her kill herself,
and that reason is one that I,
wearing my daily mask of horror, will never understand/ perhaps,
if you are born beautiful,
you are allowed to be
a fool?
And even win prizes for it?
While those of us
in our round-mouthed, deep-eyed masks
must survive,
because actually, no one would care
if we did not.

This story didn't really come out as I expected it to.
I haven't been able to make you understand what it is like
to love beauty,
yet be clothed in fat,
to have an ugly face,
not to be witty, athletic, or elegant,
only to have some obsession for truth and history,

to want to show things as they
more completely are,
not even to be skillful,
or rich,
or even a brilliant person;
to be common,
and thus feel more different than everyone who is
lucky
or beautiful
or brilliant,
or even loved;
to be common
and thus unnoticed by all.
I want to tell you
that beauty itself
creates
injustice,
and that while everyone suffers,
only beauty is allowed any mercy
from the suffering.
I have said it before,
the ones who need love most
are the unlovable.
And how much more difficult to be ugly and sensitive and still to
    survive?

In our pain, we burrow down,
and sometimes bring out grotesque horrible beauty.
Kate said that blood is like melted rubies;
but how do you melt a ruby
without volcanic upheaval that might destroy the world?

I am screaming all of this at the door,
and you are privileged to say
it is in "bad taste."
But the simple fact is that I am an old woman who has survived
    much pain,
and I want to say to that beautiful girl,
that moonstone or opal or milky glass of Pernod,
that even if she is beautiful
she shouldn't buy fools' arguments about life.
Whether her parents understand her or not
(can parents ever understand children?)
they will love her, everyone,
even her lover
will love her, and I suppose she will say
(as did that lady poet in question) that too much love can kill you;

and I will only reply,
we all have to die. Better from too much love,
than none.

Better from beauty, than
the pain of none.
That mask on the wall
shows horror.
Not at life, but its perversions.
Inside,
I am shaped like a beauty,
the blood in my veins,
thank you, Kate,
is melted rubies.
It is for the upheaval of life, for persistence,
a more complex beauty,
that we twist and strain.

A poem in response to Rexroth, Irish coffee, a day alone, forgiving men, for they have no wombs, no treasury, no sense of the infinite possession of self

to the librarian

                silver
                crystal
                light
                momentum
the blossoms of spring's flowering trees
fall on water,
float away;
some are worked into the ground, but all
pass through the mind,
a sprinkling of fragrance
on one more year
of passing.

This is a gesture of forgiveness
and love.
My martini glass reflected its Juniperian
light on the pages of your poems
today
at lunch, Mr. Rexroth. And as I read,
some peace, like the vision of all the constellations on a clear night,
passed over
me.

And you, M, dangerous scorpion,
sometimes betrayer, I
thought of you, too,
with sorrow,
with compassion,
with sad love for your need to flash
your hips to other men. We
slept so tightly together,
but, of course,
were only two small children
hugging in the garden of paradise,
holding each other
for poetry,
and some joy
we've neither
been able to describe.

Bob, this poem is for you,
Golden,
a touch of the prince,
lover of books
and rare manuscripts,
with neat hands,
which turn each page precisely,
mostly, with love.

I sit here in the precession of the equinoxes
and want to remember
the original zodiac was only the lion,
scorpion, ibex (the stars around aquarius were thus represented),
and bull.
Primal animals.

And now most of the scorpion should be called Ophiuchus, the
    Serpent Holder,
for the sun spends three weeks there,
and at last
I look for a man
in my life,
not another primal animal.

I have invented a sign of the zodiac for you:
it is called LIBRUS,
the man of books,
and everyone I love is born under the sign, for
it is a scattering of stars,
a shower of crystal
through all nativities,
looking for those whose hands
are willing
to touch
rain
or waterfall
or, in fact, the
rough
rough
crystal of life.

A welder constructs my zodiac
and offers me a mask
against the glare he creates
in drawing my map.
My hand goes up to each
shining star. Old Regulus I am,
but I look for new bodies
of light.

And in my palm, I hold
dangerous energies.
An amateur astronomer and
professional goddess.
I want to be
above all
the magician's assistant.
Watch me now,
        a star in the palm/ a
        play on your name, presto,
who are the great astronomers?
The ones who
understood naming?
And the magician,
who is he?

For I am only
the assistant. Loving the shower
of sparks
each act of love/ magic
lets rain down
on me.

The magician without the powers of the sun

What if I could turn you
into a tree?

A Brazilian floss-silk tree?

reminding me of yr
hair
which touches my face in the night
as if a tiger
had approached the bed,
his paw a softness,
his cat-like body
not hungry or mean in the
darkness.

What if your body sprouted thorns
as the trunk of this tree has,
as if there were tender ruddy points
ready to protect you
from a tight embrace?

What if I fell in love with the rain
when you were flirting
someday
reminding me
that to turn you

into a tree is not to change
yr nature
            or mine

What if danger was a silk blanket
and covered you at night?
if the floss
of my smile, like a new ear of corn,
draped over your face in the dark

if your mustache
were flossy and delicate
as corn silk
and hovered over me in the night?

What if Brazil were not on the map
and your name spelled a border to an old country
and then what if I had the powers
of magic
and could transform your indifference to love?

What if I could turn you into a tree?
And forget my own ten branches
which reach out
for love,
        for sun,
                    some flamenco dancer with a bristly
                    mustache?

A valentine for Ben Franklin who drives a truck in California

I cut the deck
and found a magician
driving a mack truck
down the California grapevine.
His eyes were glistening Japanese beetles,
and his hands were surveyors of the moon.
He pulled a carnation
out of his sleeve,
and offered me a ride.
I took the flower and said I was leaving
to be an illusionist. He said
he specialized in cards
and sleight of hand.
I touched his mouth and ears
with my lips,
               "Keep on truckin,"
I said.
But he laughed and told me a bedtime story.
His body was an elm.
His mouth was filled with grapes.
His hands turned my body into new honey.

Now I am home alone,
reading directions
for sawing a beautiful woman in half.
First you start with a mirror. . . .

Before I turn down
the crisp sheets of my bed,
I shuffle the tarot deck.
But the magician is missing.
Is he
still driving the freeways of California?
Or is he
only an illusion
in my own
magician's
head?

III

Extending the moon's complicated geography

Looking for the bald eagles in Wisconsin

a letter from the Midwest

We rode
our black camels
down to the Mississippi
at Cassville
where a sewage disposal plant
keeps America's
Bald Eagles
alive.
There are some
      cynics
      bar-fighters,
      owners of whore houses
      and tired American sheriffs
who would question
this mode
of transportation.
But we'd been eating kibbee and hoummous
stuffed eggplant, yoghurt,
and even mamouls
      (tho the dark Lebanese
      who led our caravan
      was sneaking
      Snickers bars
      in between)

and we knew
winter snow
was an illusion, a trick,
like the moon & its eclipses
to make us believe
we were not fully
alive.

Camels are mean and stubborn,
just like some men
I know,
but I'm always a sucker
for "machismo"
whether it steps down off a cranky
horse, wears
a bearskin,
or lives in a desert, solitary
and studded with saguaro.

We looked over the corn stubble
                                     crusted
with crystal snow,
saw rough-legged hawks in their
light phase
circling low over one spot;
this journey to the eagle feeding ground
was one that occupied
a large part of
the map.
No one
but you, in Eau Claire,
questioned our camels,

black,
heavy-coated against
the winter snow.

America destroyed
her own bison
and all the passenger pigeons; are now doing-in the water and
  air.
The old Americans,
that is,
and now it is up to us
to invent new animals,
new elements.
                My black camels
take me thru cornfields
as easily as desert, mountain, or
city street. I am often
tempted
to say
I'm a lost pilot,
like one of my brothers,
or that I cannot read
the best maps.
                But everyone
who knows me,
whether translating ancient tablets
or attending ceremonies for shaking
the pumpkin
would know that to be a lie. I am
a good navigator
thru any world where I can ride
those magical beasts.

My reins are made of all the phases of the moon,
the breath of hawks,
the wintry pane
of glass,
my journeys, my passages,
with my hands full of mushrooms
and red snapper,
are some dedicated search—
        to find all beauty,
        to sing all songs,
        to find
        like some mythical goddess
        a satisfaction,
        a fulfillment,
        a partner, another rider
        of black camels
        for these trips.

Eagles.
Dark with very white heads.
Sitting on the frozen river.
Sitting on the trees over the open water
where the ice had cracked.
Bald eagles.
We'd found them.
Could now turn around
and go back.
America, I
don't know who you are,
but now I've seen your totem.
Sitting on an ice floe
in the January Mississippi.

Big dark birds
dependent
on the weather
for their survival.
And how I've pulled my long hair
like a curtain
across my face and shown them the moon,
a water lily
in a dark pond, and when
they did not care
for that landscape
I've drawn the silver-threaded curtain
and changed the scene,
this time to show a moon
like the rising moon we saw,
returning from our journey to
the bald eagles' place.
It rose,
like an image in a Japanese print,
like a bloody hand,
like a red lantern in a paper house,
like a wound in a lion,
or a sunflower having been dipped
in some tiger's blood;
a hive of angry bees in a big sky.
But the landscape of the moon
is still not part of real
life; the most time
any astronaut has been gone
is a few days.
And I wonder about all these silver
capsules.

                    Perhaps
my black camels
take me farther,
carry me
more slowly and sensuously,
allowing me to collect feathers, rocks,
flowers, seashells and bleached bone
on my trips.

I know a man who drives the sphinx
to work,
and one who keeps
a Ferrari.
I once rode a zebra
and have friends, with their snow dogs,
who travel by sled.
A few skin divers tell me their
journeys are deep, down
the ladders of the ocean, past the lies of non-watery
world.
And I know woodsmen
who walk, as well as motorcyclists
who barely escape
breaking their necks. Some singers
beg for Porsches and Mercedes-Benz.
Surely some of my friends have turned into
wolves and howl in harmony
with other wild creatures.
So when you question
this shaggy black camel I ride
I sigh and wonder
why don't you trade in your Olds-
mobile?

Not for my vehicle
(for I change every year)
or for that of some other rider.
We must all invent
our own journeys,
our own transportation.

I will come to your boating party
anytime.
Men and women learn from each other,
not to trade roles,
but to share
our own fantasies,
to sometimes take each other
for an un-
traditional
Ride.

NOTE: My joke—to refer to a poem by Sam Hamod that refers to a poem of mine, mentioning other poets, mainly by their titles: Michael McClure, via Janis Joplin, Jim Harrison, Bill Merwin, C. K. Williams, Michael Dennis Brown, Dan Gerber, Tony Crea, Robert Duncan, Jerome Rothenberg, Armand Schwerner, Ed Abbey, Howard McCord, Jim Tate, and of course Sam Hamod, whose poem denouncing the black camels which I mention in my poem *Rescue Poem,* from *Inside the Blood Factory,* inspired me to respond. With references, of course, to Walter and Mary Hamady, who took me to see the eagles at Cassville, Wisconsin.

IV

Tributes and transcendencies

The last poem of the year,
written in an airport

for M

You said it was
yr last.
         You must have been thinking of leaving
even then.
For whatever else the moon is,
it is poetry in all of
our lives.
Yr anger
at yrself for failure, the Borsalino you wanted
but wd never have had the nerve to wear,
haunting around
after glamorous figures, hoping I wd turn out to be
a talisman
like an amber bee
in yr pocket/ and I
only loving you
not caring about
success or failure (foolishly/ for I failed too;
you did not believe my love).

Across from me in this giant airport,
a father and daughter play cribbage over the red carpet of
    American.
In vinyl seats, they shuffle cards, move their pegs of credit.

She has frizzy yellow hair, like Little Orphan Annie,
a baby face, and a pearl necklace above her knitted blouse.
He looks like California or Las Vegas.
In a white safari suit,
well-polished boots.
I notice she is wearing a ring,
like a wedding band, on her marriage finger,
and while he does look old enough to be her father, he is
one of those dandies who goes in for young
women.

She looks bored with the card game.
My mind wanders and I think of playing cribbage
with my father
when I was nine or ten,
and I begin wondering how the game is played
for I've forgotten/ over the years.
A litany of
fifteen-two, fifteen-four, fifteen-eight,
begins to come back,
but what are we counting points for?
And how do you score and win?

I think of you, M, who left me for a life
with other men,
just as my father left me for
aircraft carriers filled with men and planes,
a war that had to be won,
and more cribbage games with his cronies—
all men.

Across the way,
the cribbage players have put away their board
and the cards, which are black,
bearing pictures of a pink nude woman;
from out of the next chair,
behind a flight bag,
the girl
(daughter?)
takes out a bouquet of white and yellow flowers.

Baby's-breath hovering around the edge.
Yellow satin ribbons.

No,
it couldn't be a bridal bouquet.
And if it is
do you think it is hers?

This girl—
I look again.
How old is she?
Twelve?
Twenty?
Surely no more.
And how old—is it age which made me think them father and
    daughter?—
is he?
        with big silver ring,
        like the proverbial brass knuckle,
        on his little finger.
        No wedding band.

I sit here baffled.
Wanting to ask them—
                    the cribbage players—
who they are.

Father and daughter?
Husband and wife?
Strangers in an airport who are bored?
Cribbage better than nothing?

Waiting in the lounge
for a flight back to a beautiful southern beach
I think of you, whom I love so much,
and wonder about all of the
terrible discrepancies
of existence.
Maybe there is only one *terrible* fact, tho;
that none of us can choose what it is
we'll be stuck with.

A new year is going to happen
every 365 days.

Our calendar—
                    which disregards the moon—
is a reminder.
The passage of time itself disregards
event.
Or that event,
each specific reality,
that which defines each of our lives,
is irrelevant to time and perhaps even history
itself.

What does it matter
how the frizzy baby-faced blond
and her safari-suited daddy really relate,
or what event that spraying bouquet
represents?
Whether Time is not Father Time, but Lover Time?

Except to me, the speaker,
You, the reader,
All of us who care about recording poetry (our lives).

Memory:
the bee preserved in amber
that once buzzed around your head.
I will always love you.
It doesn't change,
even tho we record a new year.

Or I never see you
(the past)
again.

The pumpkin pie, or reassurances
are always false, though we love
them, only physics counts

Pumpkin,
freshly scraped out of its tightly adhering
orange skin,
as if you tried to scrape
beach foam off the sand,
the seeds washed and set out for the birds on the porch,
churned in the blender, after baking to watery
pulp in the oven.
                Fresh
pumpkin
in other words,
not that bright yellow stuff
that comes in tins,
and ready to make pie.

Enter this cook:
the experienced artist who grew up
with tin cans and a cupboard with only two
spices—salt and cinnamon.
It is my first time to make a pumpkin pie
from pumpkin.
The tin can being so much cheaper,
the time required, so much less.

How do I say this:
    cooking smells,
    as the flakey crust is baked,
    and I am stirring the custard filling,
        pumpkin pulp,
        cinnamon (my spice),
        nutmeg,
        ginger,
        allspice,
        cloves,
        the delicious thick cream,
  sugar,
  eggs,
  oh good things, and I am
stirring, stirring, not allowing
any lumps,
the spices wafting out into the house and
feeling the perfume of the kitchen,
thinking that men make better cooks than women
because they have ideas about what they do,
not feeling the simple urge to fill up or provide
a meal,
stirring, stirring, thinking,
wondering what the man I love is doing,
thinking of different kinds of skills, thinking
also
of a poet who writes about music and water to-
gether,
stirring and wondering,
wondering
why this custard does not get thick,
and finally the correct amount of time being passed
and the custard seeming thicker but not as thick

as I think it should be and knowing that
when custard starts to get thick
it gets thick really fast,
right away,
so hastily, with Mercury whizzing around my heels,
pour it into the pie shell,
then think with horror, what?
if it doesn't
get thick?
And it is an hour from dinner,
lots of guests,
and not enough cream to do the whole thing again.

I wait.
Women know about waiting.
Artists know about waiting.
Lovers are the only ones who never learn
about waiting.
But even they often
have to wait.
"Please tell love to wait for me,"
says one of the great poets,
but love never waits for anybody, at least
not in the rain,
oh tears,
oh metaphors,

Anyway,
I wait.
Test the pie filling with a knife.
Not a silver one,
because this house has no silver,

I have never had silver,
but test it,
no good.
It still isn't firm.
I put it in the refrigerator.

I wait.
I take it out after anxiously waiting,
which means I didn't wait very long.
Oh, this perfect gourmet's delight,
something even the pilgrims seemed to be able to whip up,
and I in this modern house
worrying and wondering,
has poetry really informed my life?

I have not been waiting long enough.

Anxiously, I say to a lady who has been hovering around
the kitchen,
          "do you think it will set?"
She looks at me reassuringly,
as you would look at a child who wants to know
if daylight will come again,
a lady whose husband has said that pumpkin pie
in his favorite.
              (Did his mother use pumpkin out of the can?)
I now think I should have strained my
homemade pumpkin pulp through a jelly bag to get out
excess water
          oh techniques,
how they do us in

Reassuringly, my catechism is answered:
>will the pumpkin set?
>>of course
>>do you think it will be okey by dinner?
>>>of course. it will be delicious.

Of course.
Dinner. A menu I will not describe. Delicious.
Preceded by many drinks, many
appetizers, accompanied by much wine,
much laughter and flirtation,
a party occasion.

Dessert.
Pie out of the refrigerator.
Cream whipped.

THE PUMPKIN HAS SET

The pie disappears from plates. Says
my reassurer,
the lady who holds the catechism,
the one whose husband's favorite was
Pumpkin Pie,
"I didn't think it would set.
But it turned out perfectly."

Stunned,
I smile my Christmas smile at her.
I have spent the last month thinking of that.
Why did she tell me she thought the custard would set,
if she didn't think it would?

Hateful.
I am a child.
We are all children. To be reassured.
I am ready to make her my enemy.

I have been duped.
Treated as a fraud
or lied to,
de-frauded.
Religion is dead: if there is no truth in the kitchen,
where could there be truth?

And I ask all of you that question,
all of you,
if there is no truth in the kitchen,
where possibly can there be truth?
                              I expect
a betrayer in the bedroom, perhaps,
or in any other room of the house,
the helpless mechanic under the car in the garage,
the sad plumber in the bathroom.
even a hopeless fire builder or clumsy handyman.
But not the kitchen.

Women are true.
Faithful.
Honest.
Poets
speaking
committed words
through their small lives.

That was last Christmas.
I live this year
in one room,
have no kitchen,
garage,
fireplace or
bedroom.
I even share my bathroom.
Truth is lonely and unbetrayed.
My room filled this week with
the fragrance of apples and pomegranates. There is a jug
of red wine on a table,
and a thick cutting board for my loaf and cheese.
In a pot on my desk
brown milkweed pods have burst
their down;
it hangs like snow against a bare branch,
seeds spotting the white cheek like small moles.
I know where Truth is
but wonder where friendship and family have gone.
I think of the motherly woman who lied, kindly, last year, thinking
to reassure me;
wonder now at my anger,
think how easy it is to condemn,
how hard to be compassionate.

There was a man I loved.
He never ate pie.
He could not tell me he did not love me/
I did not
want to hear.

This year, this season,
I thank all my friends, for their kindness.
Still, they know
I have always lived alone
with my own pumpkin pie truth.

And poetry,
the reassurer,
          "Do you think it will set?"
     "Of course,
     it will be delicious."

V
The ring

The ring

I carry it on my keychain, which itself
is a big brass ring
large enough for my wrist,
holding keys for safe-deposit box,
friends' apartments,
my house, office and faithless car.

I would like to wear it,
the only ornament on my plain body,
but it is a relic,
the husband gone to other wives,
and it could never be a symbol of sharing,
but like the gold it's made of, stands for possession, power,
the security of a throne.

So, on my keyring,
dull from resting in my dark purse,
it hangs, reminding me of failures, of beauty I once had,
of more ancient searches for an enchanted ring.

I understand, now, what that enchantment is, though.
It is being loved.
Or, conversely, loving so much that you feel loved.
And the ring hangs there
with my keys,
reminding of failure.

This vain head full of roses,
crystal,
bleeding lips,
a voice doomed to listen, forever,
to itself.

Tearing up my mother's letters

The rain of summer thunders down past the sweet peas
trailing up the staves
of my balcony,
and I,
just returned from a journey,
am sitting among pencils and letters and checkbooks,
thinking of the pleasures of sleeping
in my own bed tonight,
wondering if my yellow roses like this rain,
for "roses," as a good poet has said, "are heavy feeders,"
and I'm wishing I were with a certain man,
let us call him "Michael," for that name is common, and as good
as any other,
but I am alone, as usual,
taking the pleasures one has in solitude,
of music and books,
letters from/to friends,
a good glass of wine,
and I notice that I write the checks first, to pay
my bills,
then I write to my mother,
from whom I am often estranged,
and that, unlike all my other pieces of mail, which I file,
as I answer (or decide not to answer), I tear up
my mother's letter
in her fine bookkeeper's handwriting,

recalling that I have always saved most friends' letters,
but always torn up family ones.

Just a note.
The rain has stopped. I
go out on the balcony to check my plants. The sweet peas
are leaning out into the night. Lightning flashes quickly,
like the pain which slithers in and out of my right knee during
cross-country drives.
I tear up my mother's letters
because she is a sad woman and has given me
the gift of her sadness.
The words so thin and determined,
reminding me of how seriously we all take our small lives.
And I am ashamed of her letters;
they could be written by me,
that part of me I could never love,
that small, frightened, even stupid part,
determined to be noticed,
when it should rejoice in being ignored.
That too-loud voice which always embarrasses me
in a quiet room.

I tear up her letters
as I have tried to tear that part
out of me.

Walla Walla, Washington

Dear T———,

So much angst in your letter. And the old windmills, like
inefficient yet still deadly lawnmower blades whirling around. I
sensed something in your letter which I've been trying for months
to make an essay out of—subject: "Is Iowa Really the Enemy?";
discussion: how MFA programs work against the poet rather than
for him; goal: to change things, since we can't get rid of those
programs.

There is a very callous kind of egocentricity required of those of
us who not only want to write poetry but want to live in the
marketplace of poetry. I expect you are suffering from not having
that callousness, that foolish egocentricity, and worse—wanting to
be a poet, not that drunkard fall guy for Johnny Carson and the
talk-show world of the poetry business. So, you must get out.
Thousands of poets-in-the-schools appearances cannot, will not make
poetry. You know that. It is *not* the only way to make a living. So,
you must get out. Let poetry be your salvation, instead of the deadly,
dreary proposition it must have become.

I know you think that is easy for me to say. As you thought what
I said about you in the APR (not the hatchet job you think;
merely the statement that you are too talented and smart to publish
before you are ready, out of connections rather than good poems,
yet you have let the system push you into doing that, and wondering
now why it does not reward you for that mistake.

But then, I must only be reopening old wounds, and I did not

107

sit down this beautiful crisp autumn morning to do anything but send love. Also an easy word. Maybe a meaningless one. I sit here in this little white small-town house the college has provided for me, across from the student health center. A young nurse in white stockings, carrying a bouquet of gladiolas, has just parked her car and is walking in. I have begun to make this place mine for the coming four months, though the house could accommodate two families, and I, alone, will knock a bit hollowly about. Still, I have gotten to love the space of being alone, even though I do not think living alone is good for people. Especially such selfish, narcissistic people as poets.

A wandering jade plant, bought from a boy getting married this week, sprawls over my already cluttered desk. On the other side, a rose cut from the garden here, yesterday, filling the water glass with bubbles of its stem-life. No ideas but in things, says you-know-who, and I begin to realize each year how lucky I was to grow up without things. Things of my own. Books, even, were library books. But I learned that (Oriental?) lesson of seeing each thing by itself, isolate in the beauty of separateness, because there simply were few things there. The symbol given, a grace of poverty.

And I wonder, as I sit here, about you and your life. What did/ does L—— mean to you if you can abandon her with the ulcer-producing life, the blackheads of pimply preadolescent poetry-in-the-schools, and the ravages of Soho artists' bars? I must confess that you have a place in my fantasy life, and when I was last in New York, I went to Mickey's new Ocean Club (is that what it's called?) on Canal Street because Ron Sukenick had said, in June, that he had seen you there. Met a poet from Iowa who knew you. No trace of you. Then returned a few weeks later, to Michigan, to find your letter. So much fury. So flailing. So slightly disoriented. I felt a stranger had written it. Then, of course, I realized that I don't really know you; that in spite of my sense of connection with you, you are a stranger. With a side I didn't dream of.

And yet, I, of all people, should certainly understand that good poets, by definition, will be misunderstood. And that no matter how long we live, we never can accept that misunderstanding. I know you feel misunderstood. Perhaps, along with everything else, I am guilty of misunderstanding, as well.

I read today that a former mayor of Walla Walla was an undertaker. There is no Audi dealer here to fix my continuingly recalcitrant car, and the only airline from which to fly out is called Cascade. I imagine a trip in a plane shaped like a barrel which is mythically hurled over a waterfall called the state of Washington. Anyway, it is peaceful and charming here, and so small that even astronomers, chemists and economics professors talk to poets. For your nurse obsession, I present this morning's poem:

Gladiolas

The nurse,
in white stockings of lily,
and maroon car of plums,
parks
across from my window,
steps out, carrying gladiolas.

Stiff, funeral flowers;
I would distrust any nurse I saw walking down the corridors
with a spray of them,
like a music stand in her arms,
towards me.
       (Difficult syntax
       of staying alive.)
Yet, I knew a man once whose passion was growing gladiolas.
He played the cello,
had a magnificent cellar full of wine,
was tall, thin, an excellent runner,
a mean drunk,
and desperately homosexual.
Last I heard, he went to Portugal
to play in some symphony.
The gladiolas were enough to make me
worry about him.

A friend once told me she thought he was the perfect husband
for me. Thus,
I knew what she thought of me,
and ever since,

110

when I see gladiolas,
I know how the world sees
me.

Stiff,
unwieldy, in the arms of some funeral director,
mourner, or the relative of a sick or dying person.
My friend, before he left for Portugal, was growing a green gladiola.
Exotic.
Still, not beautiful, as a rose, or a lily,
or a sweet pea.
And I wonder what kind of music an orchestra of gladiolas
would make.
Probably,
not the kind
I would like to hear.

yrs,
DIANE

P.S. traveling across country is a rich and meditative experience for me. I just finished reading Tom Robbins' wonderful second novel, *Even Cowgirls Get the Blues,* about a girl, born with giant thumbs, who becomes a hitchhiker. In spite of this romance, which roped me in thoroughly, I never pick up hitchhikers. Have never dreamed of hitchhiking, myself. But feel strange pangs of guilt at my extreme pleasure in traveling alone. Finally managed to sing about it. As follows.

The hitchhikers

They burn you
like the berries of mountain ash in August,
standing by the road,
clearly defined,
Autumnal brilliant, heads
scorched from waiting
in the sun.
How can
you pass them up?
But you do,
and dream each night of a hell,
where you are a hitchhiker,
and no one will ever stop to pick you up.

Excuses:
      I'm a woman alone;
      I'm moving all my books;
      I need the time for thinking;
      One of them might murder me;
but really, it is the look each one gives me
of need,
desperate need,
pick me up, or I'll fail to reach my goal,
and that need frightens me,
so I look away,
speed on,

dream each night of a mountain ash
with its bunches of orange berries gleaming
like the failures of my life,
burning beautifully on the tree,

Oh, hitchhikers, hitchhikers,

And they remind me
that I drive across country often, looking for your face
in each car I pass,
or which passes me, knowing you would not hitchhike, either,
thinking of the two years I spent with you,
reliving them over and over,
knowing I had everything I wanted,
but like Midas was silent and stiff with the gold I had touched,
felt always as if I had been buried under a ton of diamonds,
still feel the dust of them glinting on me as I drive across country,
my hair sparkling with the brilliance you left,
and those hitchhikers,
reminding me of hell. That I had what I wanted once,
and lost it,
failed, watched myself failing,
still not understanding why I failed,
but knowing I did,
and still passing—65, 75, 85 miles an hour,
those hitchhikers,
burning by the side of the road,
burning
like the berries of the beautiful mountain ash,
burning like my tongue
on fire,
burning me, as I sleep protected in my rings of fire,
the gleaming car which hurtles me through America,

and all I have
is not enough.

Mountain ash, not the ash from out of which a bird
with glinting neck feathers who flies suddenly up on the road
in front of the swift car, would come,
not the ash on the foreheads of holy sinners,
not the ash of immortality.

Ash—a tree, with its berries not the colour of any jewel,
not the colour of blood, but a rare and exceptional colour, given only
to plants,
and I see each one of you,
as I pass on the road,
burning like the autumn berries,
and the beauty makes me pass by quickly.

In my car, is an altar, sacrificial stone and knife,
the tears of blame and understanding,
and blood; all the blood my body has lost;

Oh, hitchhikers, hitchhikers,
you would not want to travel with me.
You would not want to travel with me.

My neighbor sees the blue cineraria dazzling through my office
door,
as sky over the brown prairie makes you want to reach up and touch
  it;
she thinks it is an African violet,
for that is the only blue flower she knows the name of.

I hated my mother's silences.
The blue sky over desert or prairie. Their brownness.
Or, I thought I did.
Actually, I hated the talk more,
her ugly high voice,
her false daintiness,
her bitterness which always gave her an edge on everyone she
talked about. I hated her loud voice,
loud to me because I was like an empty room,
or the open prairie,
a desert,
where the words carry and sound big
even from small humans.

Now,
my own silences
are never big enough to make up for the foolish talk,
but I think of blue sky like a piece of turquoise against a
Navajo's skin

Those silences which sit in my life
like this cineraria
my neighbor did not know the proper name
for.

The photos

My sister in her well-tailored silk blouse hands me
the photo of my father
in naval uniform and white hat.
I say, "Oh, this is the one which Mama used to have on her
    dresser."

My sister controls her face and furtively looks at my mother,
a sad rag bag of a woman, lumpy and sagging everywhere,
like a mattress at the Salvation Army, though with no holes or tears,
and says, "No."

I look again,
and see that my father is wearing a wedding ring,
which he never did
when he lived with my mother. And that there is a legend on it,
"To my dearest wife,
        Love
        Chief"
And I realize the photo must have belonged to his second wife,
whom he left our mother to marry.

My mother says, with her face as still as the whole unpopulated part
    of the
state of North Dakota,
"May I see it too?"
She looks at it.

I look at my tailored sister
and my own blue-jeaned self. Have we wanted to hurt our mother,
sharing these pictures on this, one of the few days I ever visit or
spend with family? For her face is curiously haunted,
not now with her usual viperish bitterness,
but with something so deep it could not be spoken.

I turn away and say I must go on, as I have a dinner engagement
    with friends.
But I drive all the way to Pasadena from Whittier,
thinking of my mother's face; how I could never love her; how my
    father
could not love her either. Yet knowing I have inherited
the rag-bag body,
stony face with bulldog jaws.

I drive, thinking of that face.
Jeffers' California Medea who inspired me to poetry.
I killed my children,
but there as I am changing lanes on the freeway, necessarily
    glancing in the
rearview mirror, I see the face,
not even a ghost, but always with me, like a photo in a beloved's
    wallet.

How I hate my destiny.